T0368449

Civics Matter | 101 Workbook

Protecting Diversity and Democracy

Michelle D. Mardenborough

1 VOTE COUNTS

Protecting Diversity and Democracy

WestBow Press books may be ordered through booksellers or by contacting:

WestBow Press
A Division of Thomas Nelson & Zondervan
1663 Liberty Drive
Bloomington, IN 47403
www.westbowpress.com
844-714-3454

ISBN: 978-1-6642-9120-1 (sc)
ISBN: 978-1-6642-9121-8 (e)

Print information available on the last page.

WestBow Press rev. date: 03/21/2023

WESTBOW
PRESS®
A DIVISION OF THOMAS NELSON
& ZONDERVAN

1 Vote Counts | WORKBOOK

LEVEL ONE
CIVICS Matters~101

Protecting Diversity and Democracy

1votecounts.org

Brief Overview

Have you ever wondered what government is, what defines a government, and what is the function of a government? These are significant questions because the government plays a massive role in our daily lives. Whether we like it or not, the government is highly influential and determines almost everything in society. In the simplest terms, *"a government is an entity, typically a group of people responsible for providing leadership, rulership, or administration over a given territory."* But of course, this definition tells us nothing about what a government actually does or how it actually functions.

The Civics 101 Workbook delivers a fundamental understanding of the history and framework of the United States government on both the national and local level. The workbook will provide insight on how politics govern and shape our lifestyles and communities.

We will learn the role and responsibility of being active citizens who bring individual and collective power, to the electoral process through community engagement, accountability, and the power of the vote. The United States expects its citizens to engage and participate in the electoral process. In order to exercise democratic rights properly, people should be informed and as knowledgeable as possible.

The better educated and informed about how government operates, the better decisions people will make about how government should work. After all, true democracy is a government OF THE PEOPLE, BY THE PEOPLE, AND FOR THE PEOPLE.

> **"The vote is the most powerful nonviolent change agent you have in a democratic society. You must use it because it is not guaranteed. You can lose it."**
>
> *United States Representative John R. Lewis 2020*

Satyn Nishon Geary, former GA Senate Research Analyst |
U.S. Representative John Lewis

GET INTO GOOD TROUBLE

United States Representative

John Robert Lewis

Civil Rights Activist U.S. Politician

February 21, 1940 - July 17, 2020

Served in the United States House of Representatives for Georgia's 5th congressional district from 1987 until his death in 2020.

Course Goals

1. **A**cquire basic knowledge of Civics and U.S. Government including specific names, terms, and concepts.

2. **U**nderstand how civics, legislative, congressional, executive branches, history, culture, and geography impact each other.

3. **U**nderstand the importance of active citizenship, the role of community, city, and state elected officials and the responsibility of individual accountability.

4. **D**evelop informed forward thinkers who are committed to positive, productive, change in the community.

5. **P**repare individuals for advanced civic courses in how to run for an elected office and manage a political campaign.

CONTENTS

INTRODUCTION

1 VOTE COUNTS INC. is committed to Inspiring, Empowering, Educating, and Engaging our most vulnerable citizens on the significance and role of all citizens in the electoral process. We understand that knowledge is power therefore, 1 Vote Counts is committed to educate, engage, and empower the youth, reentrants, and our underserved community on the imperativeness of becoming an active, accountable citizen.

Our goal is to build civic strength and power in our backyards. This power can only be realized through a prioritization of understanding government and civics. We must totally comprehend our constitutional rights and the foundation of the government we reside in. We must understand the different branches of government, how a bill becomes law, the role of a political party, and the electoral process. It is imperative that we shift the mindset, awaken the dormant, and assert our political power. **It is time we realize that politics is not a bad word.** We believe when all individuals are informed on issues that negatively impact their neighborhoods, they utilize the vote to make a positive change.

Be truthful, have you ever said, "I'm not into politics; elected officials don't care about me or my community, so why should I vote for them?" If so, you are amongst millions of US citizens who feel the same way and have completely checked out of the electoral process.

However, by checking out of the electoral process you have thrown away your political power.

What is meant by political power?

Political power simply means that an individual or group of people hold the overall authority in a nation's government. Political power can be a positive, influential force for the greater good of all people. Political power can also be used for unethical, unlawful means such as mismanagement of resources and exploitation of certain people. When you willingly relinquish your right to vote, you relinquish your personal political power.

Although the American population has steadily progressed bringing civil liberties to the forefront of our everyday lives there remains centuries of systematic oppression which breeds a sense of hopelessness.

However, when we disconnect ourselves from the electoral process, and choose passivity over engaged action, we surrender our choice and suppress our voice. We relinquish all opportunity to participate in positively changing our communities and inadvertently participate in self-suppression. Voter suppression is intentional whether it is systematic or subliminal.

Your Voice and Vote Matters

The truth of the matter is politics is an all-encompassing part of life regardless of your ethnicity, your socioeconomic background, your sexual orientation, or your religious affiliation. Therefore, at the end of the day, you should be a part of the daily decisions that shape your family, your lifestyle, and your local municipality.

Your viewpoint, voice, and vote matters; I hope this workbook helps you decide to educate yourself on state and local issues and become politically engaged and active. Most importantly, I hope this workbook encourages you to **Register to Vote**, **Get Out to Vote** and realize that **Your Vote Counts!**

PRE-ASSESSMENT

There are three sections to this assessment. Answer all questions to the best of your ability! Take your time and read all the questions very carefully.

Section 1: Matching

Match the right definition to the subject on the left side. Place the correct letter on the blank beside each number.

_____ **1.** Declaration of Independence	**A.** Executive, Legislative, Judicial
_____ **2.** Political Party	**B** Years the President serves
_____ **3.** Three Branches of government	**C.** Highest court of the land
_____ **4.** Thirteen	**D.** A division of a city or town
_____ **5.** Precinct	**E.** Government by the people
_____ **6.** Civics	**F.** The study of human rights and the role of citizens, the government, and the environment
_____ **7.** Democracy	**G.** The National Anthem
_____ **8.** Four	**H.** A group of people with common interests who organize to win elections and, influence government policy
_____ **9.** Star Spangled banner	**I.** Number of original colonies
_____ **10.** Supreme Court	**J.** The founding document of the United States

Section 2: Fill in the blank

Please write the correct word on the line to complete the sentence. The words are provided for you below.

1. The _____ is the Commander-in-Chief of the United States.

2. By participating in an election, you fill out a ballot to _____.

3. There are three levels of government in the U.S.: _____, _____, and _____.

Word Box	**judicial**	**provincial**	**legislative**
	president	**municipal**	**executive**	**vote**

Section 3: Multiple Choice

Please complete each question by circling the BEST ANSWER possible.

1. The person who represent specific **congressional districts** within a state is a_____.

a) **Voter**   b) **State Representative**

c) **Democracy**   d) **U.S. Congressperson**

2. Every _____ years there is a Presidential election held in the U.S.

a) **3**   b) **4**

c) **8**   d) **2**

3. The United States system of government is called a _____, means that all people have a say in who becomes our leader.

a) **oligarchy**   b) **socialist**

c) **democracy**   d) **monarchy**

4. A group of people who have the same opinions about issues affecting Americans is called a _____.

a) **group**   b) **political party**

c) **parliament**   d) **vote**

5. The political system by which a country or community is administered and regulated is a _____.

a) parties   b) municipality

c) government   d) democracy

6. The famous protest by colonists who objected to a British tax on tea in 1773.

_____.

a) members of Parliament   b) Boston Tea Party

c) conservative Movement   d) all of the above

7. A set of rights established by law that protect the freedoms of individuals from being wrongly denied or limited by governments.

a) human rights   b) personal rights

c) civil rights   d) bill of rights

8. The two major political parties in the United States, are the_____ and the _____.

a) Tea Party   b) Democratic Party

c) Republican Party   d) Libertarian party

9. The leader of a municipal/local government is called a _____.

a) Mayor   b) Prime Minister

c) District Attorney   d) City Councilman

10. How many justices are on the Supreme Court?

a) 3   b) 4

c) 9   d) 12

Week One | My Voice Matters

Why Should I Vote?

It is easy to become disengaged or to simply ignore politics. However, it is important to focus on all the reasons you should vote. You should vote because voting is a fundamental process and right of yours to decide who best represents you. Voting keeps our system of democracy and leadership working on our behalf. Through the elections process, you can decide on what is important to you and your local community. Voting is not just your right as a U.S. citizen, it is your responsibility. Elections and voting are opportunities to make your voice heard. Whenever you vote, you do just that! Voting is important for everyone, but especially in underserved, marginalized communities. Elections make sure the issues that we care about and affect us are a part of the conversation.

Therefore, we cannot remain silent. Your vote and your voice are powerful weapons to affect and create positive change. But change will not just happen, we must come together and fight for the change we want to see in our communities. However, how can you fight a systematic process you know nothing about? That is just it, you cannot.

In order to win a fight, you must know your contender and you must have a strategic plan to win. Reading up on the issues, the candidates, and researching the ballot is your responsibility. This responsibility should not be taken lightly, because it determines your strategy and your voice. Your voice in unison, with others can change the direction of a community, state, nation, and even the world. Therefore, you must be educated and engaged in the electoral process which begins with understanding the basics of civics. Political knowledge is an important precursor for overall civic engagement. Individuals who know more about government are more likely to vote, hold elected officials accountable, participate in civic activities and run for elected office. So, start today, learn to fight, and protect democracy by educating yourself on the fundamentals of civics.

Assignment 1 | My Voice Matters

Fill in the Blank

1. You should vote because voting is a _____process and _____of yours to decide who best_____you.

2. Voting is not just your _____it is your _____.

3. Elections make sure the _____we care about and _____ are a part of the_____.

Select the Correct Answer

4. Voting keeps our system of _____ working on our behalf.

   a. **social service**

   b. **democracy and leadership**

   c. **democrats and republicans**

   d. **senators and representatives**

   e. **rich and poor**

Essay Question

5. What affects change and why?

_____

_____

_____

_____

_____

_____

Week Two | Civic Engagement

What Is It?

Civic education encompasses all the processes that affect people's beliefs, commitments, capabilities, and actions as members of the community. Civic education is concerned with three different elements: **civic knowledge, civic skills, and civic disposition**.

Civic knowledge refers to citizen's understanding of the workings of the political system and of their own political and civic rights and responsibilities (i.e., the rights to freedom of expression and to vote and run for public office, and the responsibilities to respect the rule of law and the rights and interests of others). **Civic skills** refer to one's ability to analyze, evaluate, and defend positions on public issues, as well as use their knowledge to participate in civic and political processes (i.e., to monitor government performance, or mobilize other citizens around particular issues). **Civic dispositions** are defined as the citizen traits necessary for a democracy (i.e., tolerance, public spiritedness, civility, critical mindedness, and willingness to listen, negotiate, and compromise). **Civic engagement** involves working to make a difference in the civic life of your community and developing the combination of knowledge, skills, values, and motivation to make a difference or a positive change. It also means promoting the quality of life in a community, through both political and non-political processes.

Civic engagement includes both paid and unpaid forms of political activism, environmentalism, and community service. Volunteering, national service, and service-learning are all forms of civic engagement. Civic engagement is participation in community dialogue, problem-solving, decision making, and development. Activities can be political or non-political in nature. Examples include local clean-ups, membership in community associations, voting, census participation, peaceful protests, and civil disobedience.

Assignment 2 | Civic Engagement

1. Define Civic Engagement

_____

_____

_____

2. List three forms of Civic Engagement

a.)

b.)

c.)

3. Civic engagement includes both _____ and _____ forms of political _____, _____, and _____.

4. Define Civic Disposition

_____

_____

_____

Circle the Correct Answer

5. Activities can be political or non-political in nature. Examples include

a) census participation   b) local clean-ups   c) peaceful protest

d) civil disobedience   e) voting   f) all the above

Section 4: Short Answer

Select any **Two questions** to answer. Provide as many details as you can in your answer.

1. Explain the role of a Community Activist. What do they do?

_____

_____

_____

_____

_____

2. Describe ONE way that the government impacts your life as a citizen.

_____

_____

_____

_____

_____

3. Pick ONE right that you know about. What is it? What does it mean you are allowed to do? What is the responsibility that goes along with it? How does this right affect your life?

_____

_____

_____

_____

4. Our system of government is a democracy meaning that people have a right to vote for our next leader. If you had the chance what is one thing you would ask the government to change?

_____

_____

_____

_____

Week Three | The Declaration of Independence vs The U.S. Constitution

What is the difference between the Declaration of Independence and the U.S. Constitution?

In short, the **Declaration of Independence** states that the United States of America is a country, independent of England, and includes a list of grievances against the king of England, while the **U.S. Constitution** formed our federal government and set the laws of the land.

Is the Declaration of Independence older than the U.S. Constitution?

The Declaration of Independence dates back to **1776** and is older than the U.S. Constitution. The document was finalized on **July 4** of that year, although it was not officially signed by representatives from all the thirteen colonies until **August 2, 1776.** The U.S. Constitution was not finalized until **September 17, 1787**, at the Constitutional Convention.

Thomas Jefferson was the principal drafter of the Declaration of Independence and went on to serve as the third president of the United States. **James Madison,** who is considered the "Father of the U.S. Constitution," would go on to serve as the fourth president of the United States.

The Difference Between the Preambles

The preamble to the Declaration of Independence begins with the famous sentence: **"We hold these truths to be self-evident, that all men are created equal, that they are endowed by their Creator with certain unalienable Rights, that among these are Life, Liberty, and the pursuit of Happiness."**

The U.S. Constitution begins with "We the people of the United States of America," which is notable because it shows that the Constitution is "of the people, for the people, and by the people of the United States."

Why It Matters?

The Constitution outlines the ideals of American government and describes how they should be achieved. It tells you what your rights and privileges are. The Constitution affects you, your family, and your friends as much today as it affected those who wrote it more than two hundred years ago.

What Is It?

The Constitution is the basic and supreme law of the United States. It prescribes the structure of the U.S. Government, provides the legal foundation on which all its actions must rest on and guarantees the rights due all its citizens.

Who Wrote It?

In September 1786 representatives from five states met in Annapolis, Maryland to discuss amending **the Articles of Confederation.** However, they quickly realized that representatives from all thirteen states would be required so they decided to meet the following year 1787 in Pennsylvania.

On May 25th, 1787, fifty-five delegates representing twelve states met in Philadelphia to write the U.S. Constitution. The state of Rhode Island declined from attending. On September 17, 1787, thirty-nine of the fifty-five delegates signed the document. The original draft replaced the Articles of Confederation.

The Articles of Confederation served as the written document that established the functions of the national government of the United States after it declared independence from England. It created a weak government that prevented the states from conducting their own foreign diplomacy. The Articles of Confederation also named the country the United States of America.

Weakness of the Articles of Federation
LACK OF POWER AND MONEY
Congress had no power to collect taxes
Congress had no power to regulate trade
Congress had no power to enforce its taxes
LACK OF CENTRAL POWER
No single leader or group directed government policy
RULES TO RIGID
Congress could not pass laws without the approval of 9 states
The articles could not be changed without the agreement of all 13 states

Although the main purpose of the Constitution is to provide a framework for government, it does much more than that. **It is the highest authority in the nation. It is the basic law of the United States.** The powers of the branches of government come from it. Similar to the American flag, the Constitution is a symbol of our nation. It represents our system of government and our basic ideals, such as liberty and freedom.

The Constitution Has Three Main Parts

1. The Preamble lists the reasons that the thirteen original colonies separated from their mother country and became an independent nation.

2. The Seven Articles of the Constitution define the duties of the three main parts of government: The articles also define the separate powers of the Federal and State government, and how to change the Constitution.

3. The Amendments An Amendment is a change or addition to the Constitution. The first ten amendments to the United States Constitution are called **the Bill of Rights.**

The Articles

Article 1: Legislative Branch: the U.S. Congress makes the laws for the United States. Congress has two parts, called "**Houses,**" the House of Representatives and the **Senate.**

Article 2: Executive Branch: The President, Vice-President, Cabinet, and Departments under the Cabinet Secretaries carry out the laws made by Congress.

Article 3: Judicial Branch: The Supreme Court decides court cases according to U.S. Constitution. The courts under the Supreme Court decide criminal and civil court cases according to the correct federal, state, and local laws.

Article 4: States' powers: States have the power to make and carry out their own laws. State laws that are related to the people and problems of their area. States respect other states laws and work together with other states to fix regional problems.

Article 5: **Amendments**: The Constitution can be changed. New amendments can be added to the U.S. Constitution with the approval by a two-thirds vote in each house of Congress (67,281) and three-fourth vote by the state.

Article 6: **Federal powers**: The Constitution and federal laws are higher than state and local laws. All laws must agree with the U.S. Constitution.

Article 7: **Ratification:** The Constitution was presented to George Washington and the men at the Constitutional Convention on September 17, 1787, Representatives from twelve out of the thirteen original states signed the Constitution.

The opening phrase of the Constitution's preamble; "We the People" was important because it highlighted the fact that the ultimate power of the new government rested with the people, rather than a king or the states.

We the People of the United States, in order

to form a more perfect union, establish justice,

ensure domestic tranquility, provide for the

common defense, promote the general welfare,

and secure the blessings of liberty to ourselves

and our posterity, do ordain and establish this

Constitution for the United States of America

Assignment 3 | The Declaration of Independence vs The US Constitution

Fill in the blank

Please write the correct word on the line to complete the sentence.

1. The _____ lists the reasons that the thirteen original colonies separated from their mother country and became an independent nation.

2. The Constitution affects _____, your _____, and your _____ as much today as it affected those who wrote it more than _____years ago.

3. Weakness of the Articles of Federation include: _____, _____, and _____.

Multiple Choice

Please complete each question by circling the **BEST ANSWER** possible.

1. The Constitution represents our system of government and our basic ideals, such as _____ and _____.

a) Liberty   b) Equity

c) Justice   d) Freedom

2. The Constitution has _____ main parts.

a) 7   b) 4

c) 8   d) 3

3. The courts under the Supreme Court decide criminal and civil court cases according to the correct _____, _____, and _____.

a) state   b) local law

c) city   d) federal

4. In September 1786 representatives from five states met in _____ to discuss amending the Articles of Confederation.

a) Washington DC

c) New York

c) Philadelphia

d) Annapolis, Maryland

Fill in the blank

Please write the correct word on the line to complete the sentence.

1. The first ten amendments to the United States Constitution are called the

_____.

2. The Constitution and federal laws are higher than _____and _____ laws.

3. Explain the difference between the Declaration of Independence and the Constitution?

_____

_____

4 . Explain why is the opening phrase of the Constitution's preamble; "We the People" important?

_____

_____

Week Four | The Bill of Rights ~ The Amendments

Bill of Rights

What Is It?

The Constitution established a strong national government and the rights of the states, but there was no mention of the rights of its citizens. Some of the delegates refused to sign the Constitution until a bill of rights was written to protect the freedom and rights of the individual. It was promised that a bill of rights would be attached to the Constitution. These would be the first changes, or amendments, to the document. James Madison proposed twelve amendments. Only ten were approved by the states.

Do You Know Your Rights?

The First Ten Amendments to the Constitution are

The Bill of Rights

Let's look at the rights and freedoms provided by each of the amendments:

Amendment 1: Freedom of Religion, Speech and the Press:

The Right to Assemble and Petition

The First Amendment might be one of the best known. It allows people to establish and practice their religion freely, and to speak their ideas and opinions. It protects the rights of its citizens to hold meetings and to petition the government. It gives the press (newspapers, magazines) the right to publish the news and ideas.

Amendment 2: The Right to Bear Arms

The Second Amendment gives all citizens the right to own guns. You have probably heard news stories about this recently. There has been much discussion about whether to limit the kinds of guns that can be sold. Also, many people want to require a background check for anyone purchasing a gun.

Amendment 3: Housing of Soldiers

When the colonies were ruled by England, people were forced to house soldiers in their homes. They would have to give them a place to sleep and meals. This amendment made it unlawful for a government to make a private citizen house its soldiers.

Amendment 4: Searches, Seizure and Warrants

This amendment protects people from law enforcement entering their home without their permission or an order from the court called a search warrant.

Amendment 5: Rights in Criminal Trials and the Rights of Property

Persons cannot be made to testify against themselves in a criminal trial. A person cannot be tried more than once for the same crime. A Person may not be deprived of their property without "due process of law," or fair procedures.

Amendment 6: Rights to a Fair Trial

This amendment requires a person accused of a crime to receive a speedy public trial by a jury. This did not happen in England during this time. People were held in jail for years before their trial and often the trial was held in secret.

Amendment 7: Rights in a Civil Trial

A civil case is brought by a person to get back property, to have a contract enforced, or to protect a person's rights. The Seventh Amendment allows a civil case to be decided by a jury trial when the amount of money involved is over $20.

Amendment 8: Bail, Fines and Punishment

The Eighth Amendment does not allow for unfair bail or fines and the use of cruel or unusual punishments. The framers wanted to eliminate the use of torture on suspected criminals or as a punishment for a crime.

Amendment 9: Rights Kept by the People

Some of the delegates thought that if a right was not listed in their Bill of Rights, it might be interpreted to mean that the people did not have that right. The Ninth Amendment protects the rights people have though not listed in the Constitution.

Amendment 10: Powers Kept by the States and the People

The rights not given to the national government are rights kept by the states or the people.

The Twenty-Seven Amendments to the US Constitution

What Is It? An amendment, in government and law, is an addition or alteration made to a constitution, statute, or legislative bill or resolution.

Brief Overview of the Twenty- Seven Amendments

1st People have freedom of religion, freedom of speech, freedom of the press, freedom of assembly, and the right to petition the Government. **1791.**

2nd People have the right to have a weapon to protect themselves. **1791.**

3rd Soldiers cannot take or live in a person's house. **1791.**

4th The government cannot arrest a person or search their property unless there is "probable cause." **1791.**

5th The government must follow the law (due process) before punishing a person. **1791.**

6th A person has the right to a fair and speedy trial by a jury. **1791.**

7th A person has the right to a jury trial for civil cases. **1791.**

8th The government cannot demand excessive bail or fines, or any cruel and unusual punishment. **1791.**

9th The Constitution does not include all of the rights of the people and the states. **1791.**

10th Any powers that the Constitution does not give to the federal government belong to the states. **1791.**

11th Citizens cannot sue states in federal courts. (**There are some exceptions**). 1795.

12th The President and Vice President are elected on a party ticket. **1804.**

13th Slavery is illegal in the United States. **1865.**

14th Every person born in the USA is a citizen. An immigrant can become a naturalized citizen. **1868**

15th All US male citizens have the right to vote. **1870.**

16th Congress can tax income. **1913.**

17th The people can elect US Senators. **1913.**

18th Alcohol is illegal. (Prohibition). **1919.**

19th All US female citizens have the right to vote. **1920.**

20th The President is inaugurated in January. Congress begins to meet in January. **1933.**

21st Alcohol is legal. Each state can make laws about making, selling, and drinking alcohol. **1933.**

22nd The President cannot serve for more than two terms. **1951.**

23rd The U.S. Citizens in the District of Columbia have the right to vote for President. **1961.**

24th It is illegal to make a citizen pay a voting fee or take a reading test to vote. **1964.**

25th If the president dies or cannot serve, the vice-president becomes president. If both die, the Speaker of the House becomes president. **1967.**

26th U.S. citizens who are 18 years old or older have the right to vote. **1971.**

27th Congress must limit when and how much its members are paid. **1992.**

Assignment 4| The Bill of Rights ~ The Amendments

1. Explain the importance of the Bill of Rights. What do they do?

_____

_____

_____

_____

_____

_____

2. Define Amendment

_____

_____

_____

3. List three Bill of Rights that holds major importance for you.

a.)

b.)

c.)

4. James Madison proposed _____ amendments. Only _____ were approved by the States.

5. Define the 4th Amendment

_____

_____

_____

_____

_____

True or False

1. Some of the delegates refused to sign the Constitution until a bill of rights was written to protect the freedom and rights of the individual.

True or False

2. The framers did not want to eliminate the use of torture on suspected criminals or as a punishment for a crime.

True or False

3. Regular people wrote the Bill of Rights.

True or False

Multiple Choice

1. Which Amendment abolished slavery?

a. 10th Amendment

b. 13th Amendment

c. 4th Amendment

2. Which Amendment gave males the right to vote?

a. 2nd Amendment

b. 15th Amendment

c. 24th Amendment

Week Five | The 3 Branches of Government

LEGISLATIVE BRANCH

The legislative branch is in charge of making laws. It is made up of **the Congress and several Government agencies**. The Government Publishing Office and Library of Congress are examples of government agencies in the legislative branch. These agencies support the Congress.

THE CONGRESS

What is Congress

Congress has two parts: the House of Representatives and the Senate. Members of the House of Representatives and the Senate are voted into office by American citizens in each state.

MEMBERS, OFFICES, AND STAFF

Qualifications

A Member of **the House of Representatives** must be at least 25 years of age when entering office, must have been a U.S. citizen for at least seven years, and must be a resident of the State in which the election occurred.

A Member of **the U.S. Senate** must be at least 30 years of age to enter office, must have been a U.S. citizen for nine years, and must be a resident of the State in which the election occurred.

How many members does each State have in the Senate and House of Representatives?

There are currently one hundred Senators, four hundred thirty-five Representatives, five Delegates, and one Resident Commissioner. Each State, under the Constitution, is entitled to two Senators, each serving a six-year term, and at least one Representative, serving a two-year term. Additional House seats are apportioned on the basis of State population.

Bicameral System

What is it

Bicameralism is a system of government in which the legislature comprises two houses. The modern bicameral system dates back to the beginnings of constitutional government in 17th century England and to the later 18th century on the continent of Europe and in the United States.

The Constitution grants Congress the power to levy taxes, borrow money, regulate interstate commerce, impeach and convict the president, declare war, discipline its own membership, and determine its rules of procedure. Under the system of checks and balances, Congress can override a presidential veto and can impeach the president.

Congress also has broad investigative powers. The Senate approves treaties and presidential nominees to the Supreme Court. Only Congress can appropriate funds, and each house serves as a check on the other. Several agencies are directly responsible to Congress, including the Library of Congress.

Executive Branch - President, Vice President

The executive branch is headed by the president, whose constitutional responsibilities include serving as commander in chief of the armed forces, negotiating treaties, appointing federal judges (including the members of the Supreme Court), ambassadors, and cabinet officials; and acting as head of state. The members of the president's cabinet are appointed by the president with the approval of the Senate. The Twenty-fifth Amendment describes them as "the principal officers of the executive departments," but significant power has flowed to non-cabinet-level presidential aides. The executive branch also includes independent regulatory agencies, government corporations, and independent executive agencies.

The Presidency

Unlike many countries with parliamentary forms of government, where the office of president, or head of state, is mainly ceremonial, in the United States the president has great authority and is arguably the most powerful elected official in the world. In addition to the formal constitutional responsibilities vested in the presidency, in practice presidential powers have expanded to include drafting legislation, formulating foreign policy, conducting personal diplomacy, and leading the president's political party. The president must be a natural-born citizen of the United States, at least 35 years old, and a resident of the country for at least 14 years. A president is elected indirectly by the people through an Electoral College system to a four-year term and is limited to two elected terms of office.

Vice President

Next to the president in rank, the vice president takes over the presidency in the event of the president's death, disability, resignation, or removal. Although the Constitution does not say much about the vice president's duties, it does specify that the vice president serves as the presiding officer (president) of the U.S. Senate. That role is mostly ceremonial, but it gives the vice president the tie-breaking vote when the Senate is deadlocked.

Judicial Branch

The U.S. Supreme Court, the highest court in the United States, is part of the judicial branch. The Supreme Court is made up of 9 judges called justices who are nominated by the president and confirmed by the Senate. The justices hear cases that have made their way up through the court system. The main task of the Supreme Court is to decide cases that may differ from the U.S. Constitution. Once the Supreme Court makes a decision in a case, it can only be changed by a later Supreme Court decision or by changing or amending the Constitution. This is a very important power that can affect the lives of many people. The Supreme Court interprets the Constitution and federal legislation. Beneath the Supreme Court are thirteen courts of appeals and 94 district-level trial courts.

Supreme Court Cases

Because the Constitution is vague and ambiguous in many places, it is often possible for critics to fault the Supreme Court for misinterpreting it. Among the most important doctrinal sources used by the Supreme Court have been the commerce, due-process, and equal-protection clauses of the Constitution. It also has often ruled on controversies involving civil liberties, including freedom of speech and the right of privacy. Much of its work consists of clarifying, refining, and testing the Constitution's philosophic ideals and translating them into working principles. On issues such as abortion, affirmative action, school prayer, and flag burning, the Court's decisions have aroused considerable opposition and controversy, with opponents sometimes seeking constitutional amendments to overturn the Court's decisions.

Assignment 5| The Three Branches of Government

Fill in the blank

1. What are the three branches of Government _____

and _____, _____.

2. Each State, under the Constitution, is entitled to _____Senators, each serving _____
term, and at least one Representative, serving a term _____.

3. Bicameralism is a system of _____ in which the legislature comprises
_____ houses.

Select the correct answers

4. **A Member of the U.S. Senate must meet the following qualifications.**

a.) US Citizen for 9 years

b.) Resident of the State where the election occurs

c.) US Citizen for 3 years

d.) College Graduate

e.) 25 years of age

5. Define the Judicial Branch of Government

_____

_____

_____

6. There are ten courts of appeals and thirteen district- level trial courts.

T or F

7. The Senate approves treaties and presidential nominees to the Supreme Court.

T or F

Week Six | How A Bill Becomes a Law

STEPS

A. Legislation is introduced

Any member can introduce a piece of legislation.

House

Legislation is handed to the clerk of the House or placed in the hopper.

Senate

Members must gain recognition of the presiding officer to announce the introduction of a bill during the morning hour. If any senator objects, the introduction of the bill is postponed until the next day.

B. Committee Action

The bill is referred to the appropriate committee by the Speaker of the House or the presiding officer in the Senate. Most often, the actual referral decision is made by the House or Senate parliamentarian. Bills may be referred to more than one committee and it may be split so that parts are sent to different committees. The Speaker of the House may set time limits on committees.

Bills are placed on the calendar of the committee to which they have been assigned. Failure to act on a bill is equivalent to killing it. Bills in the House can only be released from committee without a proper committee vote by a discharge petition signed by a majority of the House membership (218 members).

Detailed Steps in Committee

1. Comments about the bill's merit are requested by government agencies.

2. Bill can be assigned to subcommittee by Chairman.

3. Hearings may be held.

4. Subcommittees report their findings to the full committee.

5. A vote by the full committee - the bill is "ordered to be reported."

A committee will hold a **"mark-up"** session during which it will make revisions and additions. If substantial amendments are made, the committee can order the introduction of a **"clean bill"** which will include the proposed amendments. **This new bill will have a new number and will be sent to**

the floor while the old bill is discarded. The chamber must approve, change or reject all committee amendments before conducting a final passage vote.

In the House, most bills go to **the Rules committee** before reaching the floor. The committee adopts rules that will govern the procedures under which the bill will be considered by the House.

A **"closed rule"** sets strict time limits on debate and forbids the introduction of amendments. These rules can have a major impact on whether the bill passes.

The Rules Committee can be bypassed in three ways

1. Members can move rules to be suspended (requires 2/3 vote.)

2. A discharge petition can be filed.

3. The House can use a Calendar Wednesday procedure.

C. Floor Action

Legislation is placed on the Calendar

House: Bills are placed on one of four House Calendars. The Speaker of the House and the Majority Leader decide what will reach the floor and when. (Legislation can also be brought to the floor by a discharge petition.)

Senate: Legislation is placed on the Legislative Calendar. There is also an Executive calendar to deal with treaties and nominations. Scheduling of legislation is the job of the Majority Leader. Bills can be brought to the floor whenever a majority of the Senate chooses.

Debate

House: Debate is limited by the rules formulated in the Rules Committee. The Committee of the Whole debates and amends the bill but cannot technically pass it. Debate is guided by the Sponsoring Committee and time is divided equally between proponents and opponents. The Committee decides how much time to allot to each person. Amendments must be germane to the subject of a bill - no riders are allowed.

The bill is reported back to the House (to itself) and is voted on. A quorum call is a vote to make sure that there are enough members present (218) to have a final vote. If there is not a quorum, the House will adjourn or will send the Sergeant at Arms out to round up missing members.

Senate: Debate is unlimited unless cloture is invoked. Members can speak as long as they want, and amendments need not be germane - riders are often offered. Entire bills can therefore be offered as amendments to other bills. Unless cloture is invoked, Senators can use a filibuster to defeat a measure by "talking it to death."

Vote: the bill is voted on. If passed, it is sent to the other chamber unless that chamber already has a similar measure under consideration. If either chamber does not pass the bill, then it dies. If the House and Senate pass the same bill it is sent to the President. If the House and Senate pass different bills, they are sent to Conference Committee. Most major legislation goes to a Conference Committee.

D. Conference Committee

Members from each house form a conference committee and meet to work out the differences. The committee is usually made up of senior members who are appointed by the presiding officers of the committee that originally dealt with the bill. The representatives from each housework to maintain their version of the bill.

If the Conference Committee reaches a compromise, it prepares a written conference report, which is submitted to each chamber. The conference report must be approved by both the House and the Senate.

E. The President

The bill is sent to the President for review.

A bill becomes law if signed by the President or if not signed within 10 days and Congress is in session.

If Congress adjourns before the 10 days and the President has not signed the bill, then it does not become law ("Pocket Veto.")

If the President vetoes the bill, it is sent back to Congress with a note listing his/her reasons. The chamber that originated the legislation can attempt to override the veto by a vote of two-thirds of those present. If the veto of the bill is overridden in both chambers, then it becomes law.

F. The Bill Becomes A Law

Once a bill is signed by the President or his veto is overridden by both houses it becomes a law and is assigned an official number.

Assignment 6 | How A Bill Becomes A Law

1. Who can introduce Legislation?

_____.

2. Failure to act on a bill is equivalent to _____.

3. List three of the five detailed steps of the Committee.

a.)

b.)

c.)

4. The _____ may set time limits on committees. Bills are placed on the calendar _____ to which they have been assigned.

5. Define A quorum call.

_____

_____

_____

6. What is the Conference Committee; explain what do they do?

_____

_____

_____

_____

_____

7. The conference report must be approved by both the _____ and the _____

8. List the three ways The Rules Committee can be bypassed

a.)

b.)

c.)

9. Senators can use a _____ to defeat a measure by "talking it to death."

10. Explain what happens if the President vetoes the Bill

_____

_____

_____

_____

_____

_____

_____

_____

_____

_____

_____

_____

_____

Week Seven | Political Parties

The History

No political parties officially existed when the U.S. Constitution was written in 1787. The founders of the country actually felt that political parties were not a good thing and that they would divide people against each other and harm the democracy.

However, within 10 years after the Constitution was written, the U.S. had two major political parties the Federalist party that supported a strong central government and the Democratic-Republican party (also called the Anti-Federalist Party) that supported strong state governments.

The Democratic-Republican party eventually became known as the Democratic party.

The Whig party was developed in the 1830s in direct opposition to President Andrew Jackson and his policies. The Whig party eventually split apart, mainly over the issue of slavery. **Proslavery Whigs rejoined the Democratic party, and several antislavery Whigs formed a new party in 1854 called the Republican party**. Abraham Lincoln was the first Republican president.

Today there are over **420** registered political parties in the United States of America, with various blends of political viewpoints.

What is a Political Party?

A political party is an organization of voters who favor similar policies and styles of government. Parties support their candidates in local, state, and national elections. They help voters get to know the candidates by spreading their message and their positions on important issues. For well over a century, the two biggest parties in the U.S. have been **the Democrats** and **the Republicans**. The **Democratic Party was formed in the 1820s. The Republican Party was formed in 1854.**

The Difference between Republicans and Democrats

From a high-level perspective, **Republicans** tend to be more conservative, which means they generally think government should play a limited role in regulating business, the right to bear arms, and making social reforms. **Democrats** tend to be more liberal, which means they generally think government should play an active role in regulating business, provide more services to the less fortunate, protect the environment, and work towards solving social problems.

What is America's two-party system?

The U.S. is often described as having a **"two-party system"** because the Democrats and the Republicans have dominated U.S. politics since the mid-1800s. Today, almost all elected officials are members of one of those two parties. However, other political parties can promote candidates in a presidential election.

People who support the two-party system argue that it keeps our government stable. They also say that this system makes participation simpler for voters since they have to decide between only two choices. Those who oppose the two-party system argue that it limits voters' choices and prevents change. They also question whether two parties can truly represent the diverse beliefs and values in a country as big as the United States.

Are there other parties besides Democrats and Republicans?

Yes. There are many other parties, known as third parties. These parties are much smaller and not as well funded as the Democrats and Republicans. Both the **Democratic Party and the Republican Party** are recognized in all 50 states and Washington, D.C.

Three minor parties were recognized in more than 10 states as of December 2021

- o **Libertarian Party: 33 states**

- o **Green Party: 17 states**

- o **Constitution Party: 12 states**

The Libertarian Party is one of the biggest third parties. Its goals are to expand freedoms for individuals and to limit the power of the federal government.

The Green Party focuses on environmental issues and advocates environmental protection, social justice, nonviolence. and government reform policies.

The Constitution Party focuses on restoring the Federal Government to the Constitution's provisions and has the Federal Election Commission (FEC) recognized national party status.

Although there are numerous political parties in the United States, only certain parties qualify to have the names of their candidates for office printed on election ballots.

Why join a party?

Any registered voter can vote for any candidate in a general election. **However, to vote in a primary election, you may be required to belong to a party depending on where you live.** In most states, members of a political party may vote only in that party's primary. However, some states allow voters to decide which party's primary they want to vote in, regardless of whether they belong to that party—or to any party at all. Another reason people join political parties is that they want to support a group that shares their ideas. But within any political party, there are people with a wide variety of viewpoints. You don't have to share all the positions held by the party to which you belong.

Before joining a political party, you should research where the parties stand on the issues that are most important to you. Then you can decide which party, if any, most closely matches your points of view. A good way to learn where parties stand on specific issues is to read their platforms

Assignment 7 | Political Parties

1. Explain what a Political Party is.

_____

_____

_____

1(a)   List **Three** Political Parties.

_____

_____

_____

2. List two reasons why people join a Political Party.

a.)

b.)

3. _____ and the, _____ are recognized in all 50 states and Washington, D.C.

4. List three difference between Republicans and Democrats.

_____

_____

_____

5. List the three minor parties that were recognized in more than 10 states as of December 2021.

_____

_____

_____

6. The logo for the Republican party is the donkey.

T or F

7. The Whig party was developed in the 1830s in direct opposition to President Andrew Jackson and his policies

T or F

Week Eight | State and Local Government

State government is structured in the same way as the federal government but on a smaller scale. Each state has its own constitution that runs the laws of the state that are not covered by the federal government. The 10th amendment to the U.S. Constitution states that all powers not granted to the federal government are given to the states and the people. Just like the federal government, the states each have three branches of government including the **Executive, Legislative**, and **Judicial Branches**. However, no two states are exactly alike. Sometimes laws, policies, and procedures that work in one state are duplicated in another state. This tendency to implement the "best practices" of states has maintained positive operations within state government. State and local governments handle a lot of the systems that we use and encounter daily. These include schools, police departments, fire departments, libraries, parks, and more.

State Constitution

Every State has a constitution that defines the legal and political framework for government within that state. State constitutions are subjected to the highest law of the land, meaning that provisions of state constitution that conflict with supreme, federal law are deemed unconstitutional. Although state constitutions are the supreme law of the state for issues that fall outside of federal law.

Executive Branch

The head of the government in each state is the governor; other parts of the executive branch may include the lieutenant governor, attorney general, and the secretary of state. The governor is the highest elected state official and the most powerful elected official in the state. The governor's power can be divided into three categories: executive, legislative and leadership. The governors most important role is drafting an annual state budget. At the beginning of each year the governor submits a budget to the states legislature that outlines spending and policy priorities for the year as well as tax increases or cuts. Afterwards, the governor and the legislature negotiate on spending and programs until an amicable decision is made.

Legislative Branch

Exactly like the federal government the states have legislatures that make up the state laws, handle the budget, and levy taxes. Many similarities exist between Congress and the state legislature, both represent their constituents, work with executive leaders to pass laws, receive their authority from the state constitution and hold elections every two and four years. Every state but Nebraska has two houses similar to the federal government. This is called a bicameral legislature. Nebraska just has a single house. One consistency throughout all fifty states is the location of the state legislature; each convenes at the state house located in the state capital.

Judicial Branch

Most State's Judicial Branch is similar to the Federal system where there is a State Supreme Court and then lower courts below them that handle the day-to-day cases.

In **Pennsylvania**, the judiciary has four general levels.

The Minor Courts are courts of limited jurisdiction, hearing arraignments in most cases. The Minor Courts are presided over by **non-lawyer magistrates** in some instances. **The Court of Common Pleas** is the trial court of general jurisdiction. **The Superior Court / Commonwealth Court** act as intermediate appellate courts, with the Superior Court having jurisdiction over most civil and criminal matters, while **the Commonwealth Court** hears matters involving government regulations. **The Pennsylvania Supreme Court** is the highest court in the state.

What is the difference between a State and a Commonwealth?

Other than the name, there really is no legal or governmental difference between states known as states and states known as commonwealths. The word **commonwealth combines the word common and wealth (as in "the condition of being happy and prosperous") and is typically understood to imply that the commonwealth was founded through the common will of the people and for the common good.** Commonwealth was simply the word chosen as the official designation of each of them as a political entity and the one used in official founding documents such as the state constitution. In fact, the word state is also often used in such documents without any distinction. Four U.S. states are technically designated as commonwealths: **Pennsylvania** (admitted to the union December 12, 1787), **Massachusetts** (February 6, 1788), **Virginia** (June 25, 1788), and **Kentucky** (June 1, 1792). The first three were among the original 13 colonies (Kentucky was part of Virginia until it became the 15th state).

All four use the word commonwealth in their official name: the Commonwealth of Pennsylvania, the Commonwealth of Massachusetts, the Commonwealth of Virginia, and the Commonwealth of Kentucky. In addition, the states of **Vermont** and **Delaware** use both commonwealth and state in official documents.

Local Government

Below the state government is the local government. There are even separate levels of government here. At the first level is the county government sometimes these are called boroughs or parishes.

County Government is the most common jurisdiction of local government within the United States. Every state except Alaska, Rhode Island and Connecticut are comprised of county governments. Counties were modeled after the English Shire which was an administrative arm of England's national government. The colonist adopted the Shire model to govern the new American colonies. Over the years counties have assumed major authority and responsibility and have begun to provide numerous services to their residents. Today county governments are significant providers and administrators of critical government services. County governments are unique, unlike cities they are not incorporated and unlike states they have no constitutional powers. In effect a county government serves as a middleman between local and state government. Most county governments take one of three forms of government:

Commission –Referred to as "Board of Commissioners" In a commission government the elected board serves as the legislative and executive branch; it has the power to adopt budgets enact regulations set policy and appoint county officials.

Commission-Administrator – The Board appoints an administrator who serves at the board's discretion. The role of the administrator is different depending on the county. Some Administrators have a wide range of responsibilities and others have practically none.

Council Executive – A county executive is elected by the county at large and serves as the Chief Administrator with major responsibilities such as drafting budgets and oversight of all department heads.

In addition to a county executive and county legislature or commissioners; most counties have four elected positions:

County Clerk – Responsible for the official records of the county, such as birth and death certificates, mortgages, deeds and adoption papers as well as marriage, automobile and business licenses. The County clerk is usually elected to a four-year term.

Sheriff – Responsible for providing law enforcement to areas of the county that are not incorporated towns. The county sheriff's authority varies from county to county. Some are elected and some are appointed.

County Attorney – Responsible for legal representation or advocacy for the county in all civil lawsuits brought against it. The county attorney also conducts criminal investigations and prosecutes criminals.

County Assessor – Responsible for determining the value of residences within the county for tax purposes. The assessor performs reevaluations of all properties throughout the county to ensure that there is a consistent and fair tax basis.

The next level is the **city or town government**. The powers and responsibilities between counties and cities can vary widely from state to state. In some states there is almost no county government, where in others, the county is an important part and may be responsible for something as important as funding schools. For a city to be officially recognized, it must be incorporated; to be incorporated it must have a charter.

City Charter's outlines the power and structure of the government, including elections and appointments there are four types of city charters.

Home Rule – Allows residents to draft a city charter, which is then voted on and any future amendments.

General Charter – Cities are classified according to population size.

Optional Charter – Provides residents a voice to shape their government.

Special Charter – An antiquated process, provisions specific to every new city. Amendments must be passed by the State legislature.

After, incorporation a form of government must be chosen, cities have several options to choose from including the following.

Mayor Council - Also known as the Strong Mayor Government, both the mayor and a unicameral city council are elected. The city council is composed of either districts or at large members. In most situations, the mayor has the authority to veto legislation passed by the City Council, hire and fire city administrators and department heads, and draft a budget.

Council Manager - Sometimes referred to as the weak mayor form of government, under this model the city manager is a nonpolitical administrator who is responsible for running the daily operations of the city. He or she is usually appointed by the City Council and provides little leadership outside of his or her defined duties.

Commission – The Commission is the least common of the three city governments only about 100 cities nationwide use a Commission. Under this model an elected Board of Commissioners performs the operations of the city and overseas the departments and agencies. A mayor is sometimes chosen from commissioners though it's largely a ceremonial position.

Overall cities, or municipalities manage numerous services such as the police and fire departments, local courts, city taxes, public transportation, streets, signs, and city parks.

Local Politics - Local government serves as a starting point for concerned citizens who want to enter the political process. Most people seek local office out of a commitment to serve their community; others have a passion, around issues such as the economy, the environment, social justice, etc. Others use local government as an entrance to higher political office. One of the strengths of our democratic system of government is that the process is available and open to every U.S. citizen, who wants to make a difference.

All Politics is Local - Local elections may lack the attention or the participation of national, or even state races but the issues, and the decisions made by city councils, township supervisors, school boards, mayors and commissioners have a direct and immediate impact on the lives of residents in the communities they serve. When it's all said and done, all policy and legislation, touch the lives of people where they live, and work daily so don't hesitate to get involved with local elections.

Assignment 8 | State and Local Government

Section 1: Fill in the Blank

1. State government is structured in the same way as the _____ but on a smaller scale.

2. Every State has a _____ that defines the _____ and _____ framework for government within that state.

3. The word commonwealth combines the word _____ and _____ (as in "the condition of being happy and prosperous") and is typically understood to imply that the commonwealth was founded through the _____ and for the common good.

4. _____Government is the most common jurisdiction of local government within the _____.

Section 2: Multiple Choice

Please complete each question by circling the BEST ANSWER possible.

1. Select two of Pennsylvania's **four judiciary general levels.**

a) Court of Common Pleas   **b) The Minor Court's**

c) The Superior Courts   **d) The Lower courts**

2. Every _____ years there is a Gubernatorial state election.

a) 10   **b) 4**

c) 8   **d) 2**

3. The United States system of government, is called a _____ and determines that all people have a voice in the electoral process.

a) oligarchy   **b) socialist**

c) democracy   **d) monarchy**

4. A city charter outlines the power and structure of the government, including elections and appointments there are four types of city charters. _____.

Select two city charters

a) **Optional Charter**

b) **Political party**

c) **Parliament**

d) **Home Rule**

5. **Essay Question**

Why Are All Politics Local?

_____
_____
_____
_____
_____
_____
_____
_____
_____
_____
_____
_____
_____
_____
_____
_____
_____
_____

Week Nine | The Electoral Process, The Electoral College, The Popular Vote

What Is an Election?

An election is the process by which U.S. citizens select the thousands of men and women they want to run their government. In a democracy, government officials are chosen by the people and serve for a specific time called a term of office. Depending on state laws, an official may run for reelection once the term is over. Our system of government is called a representative democracy. American citizens do not directly make governmental decisions; however, they elect officials to govern for them. Most elections in our country are held on the first Tuesday after the first Monday in November. But elections for public offices may be held at any time, depending on state law.

Electoral Process Milestones

1787 - When the Constitution was written in 1787, it basically left the decision to each state as to who could vote in elections. Most states did not give the right to vote to women or African Americans.

1865 - The roots of Jim Crow laws began as early as 1865. It was named after a Black minstrel show character. Black codes were strict local and state laws that determined when, where and how formerly enslaved people could work, and for how much pay. The codes appeared throughout the South as a legal way to put Black citizens into indentured servitude, to control where they lived and how they traveled and to seize children for labor purposes.

1870 - In 1870, five years after the end of the Civil War, the 15th Amendment was passed. This amendment guaranteed the right to vote to male African Americans.

1870 - The first African American to take advantage of the new right to vote was Thomas Mundy Peterson. Peterson cast his historic vote on March 31, 1870. The iconic vote was cast in a local election in Perth Amboy, New Jersey for the town's charter.

1880 - African Americans exercised the right to vote and held office in many Southern states through the 1880s, but in the early 1890s, steps were taken to ensure subsequent "white supremacy." Literacy tests for the vote, "grandfather clauses" excluding from the franchise all whose ancestors had not voted in the 1860s, and other devices to disenfranchise African Americans were written into the laws of former Confederate states. Unfortunately, It took another 100 years for African Americans to be able to fully exercise the right to vote.

1920 – In 1920 the 19th Amendment to the Constitution was passed, and the following November millions of American women voted in the presidential election for the first time. Prior to that women were not allowed to vote at the national level.

1965 - In 1965, Congress passed the Voting Rights Act which was extended in 1970, 1975, and 1982. This law guaranteed that the federal government would intervene if any state attempted to deny a citizen's voting rights because of race. As a result of this act, millions of African Americans in the South were allowed to register to vote for the first time. The law came seven months after Dr. Martin Luther King Jr. launched the Southern Christian Leadership Conference (SCLC) campaign based in Selma, Alabama, with the sole purpose of pressuring Congress to pass Voters Rights legislation. In addition to facing arbitrary literacy tests and poll taxes, African Americans in Selma and other southern towns were intimidated, harassed, and attacked when they attempted to register to vote. On March 7th, 1965 community leaders and civil rights activists, led by then 25 year old civil rights activist, John Lewis were brutally assaulted by state troopers which subsequently attracted national attention to the civil rights movement.

The world owes a great debt to several civil rights pioneers such as:

Martin Luther King Jr, Coretta Scott-King, John Lewis, Fannie Lou Hamer, Rosa Parks, Julian Bond, Medgar Evers, Dorothy Height, James Farmer, Roy Wilkins, Whitney Young Jr, and numerous more.

1971 - The 26th Amendment to the Constitution, which was adopted in 1971, says that anyone over 18 is allowed to vote. On the average, about 60% of voting-age Americans vote in presidential elections. For local elections, voter turnout is usually much lower.

2008 - On Nov. 4, 2008, Barack Hussein Obama was elected the 44th president of the United States. The Democratic first-term U.S. Senator from Illinois would go on to mark his place in history as the nation's first Black commander-in-chief. Obama's election became a meaningful moment considering America's harsh racial history through slavery and the heavily segregated years of the Jim Crow Era, which prevented equal access and economic leverage to African Americans.

More than 131 million people cast ballots, making voter turnout for the 2008 election the highest it had been in 40 years. Obama secured 95 percent of the African American vote; 67 percent of the Latino vote; and 66 percent of votes from 18–24-year-olds. President Barak Obama was re-elected on Nov. 6, 2012, with nearly 63 million popular votes and 332 electoral votes.

2021 - Kamala Harris made history as the first female, first black, and first Asian-American U.S. Vice-President

Primary Vs Caucus

What is the difference between a primary and a caucus?

The Primary elections are run by state and local governments, while Caucuses are private events that are directly run by the political parties. Some states only hold caucuses, and others use a combination of both. At a caucus, individuals viewed favorably within the party are identified as potential delegates. After a comprehensive discussion and debate, an informal vote is held to determine which individuals will serve as delegates at the national party convention.

The Primary

State governments fund and run Primary elections the same way they do the general election in the fall. Voters go to a polling place, and vote.

Four Types of Primary Elections:

Open - Open primaries and caucuses allow all registered voters, regardless of party affiliation, to vote in any party contest.

Closed - Closed primaries and caucuses require voters to register with a specific party to be able to vote for that party's candidates.

Semi-open - Semi-open primaries and caucuses allow any registered voters to vote in any party contest. But, when they identify themselves to election officials, they must request a party's specific ballot.

Semi-closed - Semi-closed primaries and caucuses follow the same rules as closed ones, but they also allow voters who are not affiliated with a political party to vote.

The Electoral College

How was the Electoral College established?

The Constitutional Convention in 1787 settled on the Electoral College as a compromise between delegates who thought Congress should select the president and others who favored a direct nationwide popular vote. Instead, state legislatures were entrusted with appointing electors.

Article II of the Constitution, which established the executive branch of the federal government, outlined the framers' plan for electing the president and vice president. Under this plan, each elector cast two votes for the president; the candidate who received the most votes became the president, with the second-place finisher becoming vice president; which led to administrations in which political opponents served in those roles. The process was overhauled in 1804 with the ratification of the 12th Amendment, which required electors to cast votes separately for president and vice president.

What does it mean?

When you vote for a mayor, senator, a member of the House of Representatives, a judge, etc. you are voting directly for that person. However, when you vote for president, you are really voting for an elector who has pledged to represent that candidate. The electors chosen by each state are called the electoral college. They are a group of people who officially elect the president and vice president. Each state has as many votes in the electoral college as it has senators and members of the House of Representatives. In total, the Electoral College comprises 538 members. A presidential candidate must win a majority of their votes, at least 270 in order to win the election.

Although, the American public knows the winner of the presidential election on the actual day of the election in November, the winner is not official until the electoral college meets in December. Its votes are sealed and sent to the U.S. Senate. When the Congress meets in January, the current vice president of the United States unseals the envelope and announces the results to the Senate. This is the official moment at which the president and vice president are elected.

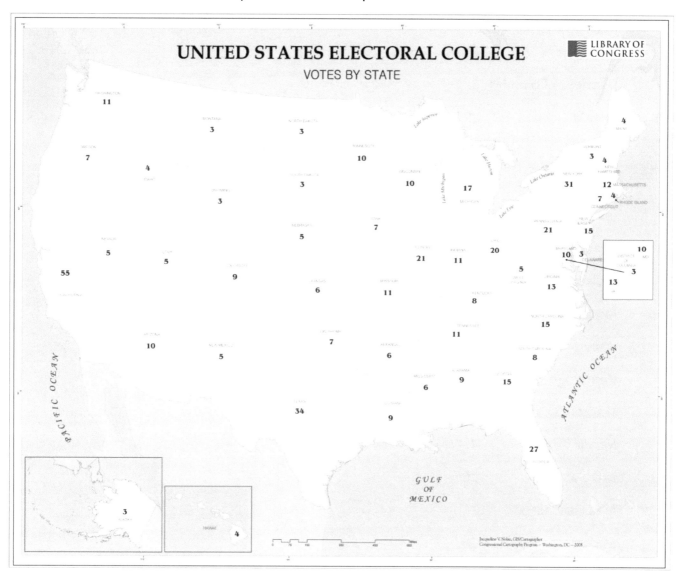

State	Electoral	Votes
•	Alabama	9
•	Alaska	3
•	Arizona	11
•	Arkansas	6
•	California	55
•	Colorado	9
•	Connecticut	7
•	Delaware	3
•	District of Columbia	3
•	Florida	29
•	Georgia	16
•	Hawaii	4
•	Idaho	4
•	Illinois	20
•	Indiana	11
•	Iowa	6
•	Kansas	6
•	Kentucky	8
•	Louisiana	8
•	Maine	4
•	Maryland	10
•	Massachusetts	11
•	Michigan	16
•	Minnesota	10
•	Mississippi	6
•	Missouri	10
•	Montana	3

- Nebraska 5
- Nevada 6
- New Hampshire 4
- New Jersey 14
- New Mexico 5
- New York 29
- North Carolina 15
- North Dakota 3
- Ohio 18
- Oklahoma 7
- Oregon 7
- Pennsylvania 20
- Rhode Island 4
- South Carolina 9
- South Dakota 3
- Tennessee 11
- Texas 38
- Utah 6
- Vermont 3
- Virginia 13
- Washington 12
- West Virginia 5
- Wisconsin 10
- Wyoming 3

What happens if No Candidate gets 270 Electoral Votes?

If no presidential candidate gets 270 electoral votes, the decision moves to the House of Representatives, which would hold what's called a contingent election in which each state gets a single vote. This means California and Wyoming get equal power, despite CA having 50 times the population of Wyoming. Each state's delegation votes in favor of the party that has more House seats in that state.

The Popular Vote

What does the Popular Vote mean in an election?

The popular vote in an election means that citizens directly elect candidates. When a voter picks up a ballot, they mark their preferred candidate's or party's name, and then ballots are counted directly.

How does the Popular Vote work?

Popular vote is a simple method of election where citizens directly vote for candidates or parties. For example, in the U.S. senators and representatives are elected by popular vote. When one votes for a senator, they select the name of their preferred candidate, the ballots are counted, and the candidate with the most votes wins (yet some states organize runoff elections between two top contenders if no candidate obtains 50% of the vote). If the U.S. president was elected by direct popular vote and not an electoral college, the process would be like a senatorial election, but on a nationwide scale.

Assignment 9 | The Electoral Process, The Electoral College, The Popular Vote

1. In a _____, government officials are chosen by the people and serve for a specific time called a _____.

2. A presidential candidate must win a majority of their votes at least _____ in order to win the election.

3. List **Four** Electoral Process Milestones

1. _____
   _____
   _____
   _____

2. _____
   _____
   _____
   _____

3. _____
   _____
   _____
   _____

4. _____
   _____
   _____
   _____

Section 3: Multiple Choice

Please complete each question by circling the BEST ANSWER possible.

1. There are Four Types of Primary Elections; circle two:

a) **Closed**   b) **Open**

c) **Democracy**   d) **Semi-together**

2. In total, the Electoral College comprises _____ members.

a) 100   b) 543

c) 538   d) 250

3. On Nov. 4, 2008, Barack Hussein Obama was elected the _____ president of the United States.

a) 40th   b) 48th

c) 42nd   d) 44th

What is the difference between a primary and a caucus?

_____

_____

_____

_____

_____

_____

_____

_____

_____

_____

Section 4: Circle Yes or No

1. A primary election is a contest to select a political party's nominee to run in the General Election.

Yes or No

2. The popular vote in an election means that citizens directly elect candidates.

Yes or No

3. Obama secured 75% percent of the African American vote; 67 percent of the Latino vote; and 95 percent of votes from 18–24-year-olds.

Yes or No

4. A General Election is a contest in which candidates are elected to office.

Yes or No

5. California and Wyoming get equal power, despite CA having 50 times the population of Wyoming.

Yes or No

6 A Caucus is a meeting held by the House of Representatives.

Yes or No

7. A presidential candidate must win a majority of their votes at least 270 in order to win the election.

Yes or No

Week Ten | 1 VOTE COUNTS

1 Vote Counts is a nonpartisan 501c3 civic engagement organization. Our goal is to educate at-risk communities, including returning citizens and, the youth on pertinent issues that will impact their future, as well as increase voters' registration and participation. This is accomplished through deep canvasing, grassroots lobbying, educational seminars, digital marketing and citizen advocacy.

Our Vision is to move toward social change that will provide true democracy; where all communities, including the underserved and returning citizens have electoral representation that will advance civic engagement. Our long-term objective is to develop a pipeline of passionate, authentic, leaders that reflect the communities they serve.

WHY VOTE?

1. **IT'S YOUR RIGHT** - The law does not require citizens to vote, but voting is an important part of any democracy. By voting, citizens are participating in the democratic process. When you vote, you take an active role in deciding issues regarding health care, equal opportunity, voting rights, infrastructure, jobs, education, social security, neighborhood safety, taxes, etc.

2. **DECIDE HOW YOUR TAXES WILL BE ALLOCATED** - Elected officials decide how to pay for public services with the money collected from our taxes and how to share the tax burden. Take an active role and find out if your candidate shares your views and will spend your money wisely.

3. **VOTE FOR FUTURE GENERATIONS** - Worried about climate change? Thinking about how you will pay off your student loans? Hoping you will have health insurance when you need it? Vote for leaders that are committed to solving these problems for you and your children.

4. **VOTE TO IMPROVE YOUR COMMUNITY** -Elected officials and judges make day to day decisions on laws that will affect your community, law enforcement, crime prevention, traffic patterns, and where to build schools, parks, and recreational places.

5. **VOTE FOR HEALTHCARE OPTIONS** - Your vote gives Governors, Legislators, and Congress the authority to pass or reject laws that will determine your access to health care. Vote and elect people who have your best interest in mind. Do it so your loved ones can have access to health care that represents your views.

6. **VOTE TO IMPROVE YOUR CHILD'S EDUCATION** - Local and state school board members who you elect make decisions on policies and budgets that will impact how well prepared your children will be for their future. Your Legislators, Governor, Congress Members, and the President also make decisions that affect the cost and quality of public schools and higher learning institutions. Vote to place your children and grandchildren in good hands.

7. **YOUR VOTE MATTERS** - Do you want someone else deciding for you the laws that will affect your family and community? Voting gives you the power to choose how your city, state, and

country will operate. If you do not vote, you cannot complain! Go vote and make the decision before someone else does it for you.

ALL ABOUT THE VOTE

Ballot

In political elections, voters are provided printed ballots and voters must check the empty box next to the person they are voting for. Some jurisdictions provide electronic monitors, which allows people to vote by clicking the box of the person's name they select.

Referendum

A referendum is when voters make a "Yes" or "No" decision on a proposal. It can be any proposed change to documents or laws. State and federal governments can use a referendum to allow voters to approve of or reject a new law, proposal, or course of action. The result of a referendum may be the adoption of a new policy or law or a change to an organization or government constitution.

Vote Early

The state of **Pennsylvania** offer's early voting You can choose whether to vote on Election Day or during the in-person mail ballot voting period, whichever is easier for you. This can be especially helpful if it would be difficult or not possible for you to vote on Election Day.

Vote In Person on Election Day

If you prefer to vote in-person at your polling place, polls are open in the state of **Pennsylvania** from 7 a.m. to 8 p.m. If you are in line when the polls close, stay in line. You are entitled to vote.

Vote By Mail

For your convenience, any registered Pennsylvania voter has the freedom to vote by mail-in ballot in an election without providing a reason.

How To Vote by Mail?

In the state of **Pennsylvania**, any registered voter can request to get a ballot by mail. There are multiple ways to request a mail ballot for the next election: online, by mail, and in person. Fill out the mail ballot application and mail or return it in person to your local election office.

Absentee Ballot

The process to request an absentee ballot is similar to that for requesting a mail ballot. You can apply online or download the form and send it to your county election office. However, the application requires you to list a reason for your absence, unlike a mail ballot.

53

Registered Pennsylvania Voters who may Vote Absentee Ballot include:

1. College students

2. Individuals whose work or vacation take them away from the municipality where they live

3. Individuals with a physical disability or illness that prevents them from going to the polling place

4. Members of the military

5. Individuals who may have a conflict due to the celebration of a religious holiday

VOTING RIGHTS FOR ALL

1. Individuals who are on probation or released on parole

2. Incarcerated individuals convicted of misdemeanors can **vote with a mail in ballot**

3. Individuals who are under house arrest can **vote with a mail in ballot**

4. Individuals being held while awaiting trial **vote with a mail in ballot**

5. Individuals on pre-release/halfway house can vote

"Stay Woke Vote"

Assignment 10 | 1 Vote Counts

Section 1: Fill in the Blank

1. A _____ is when voters make a "Yes" or "No" decision on a proposal.

2 _____ gives you the power to choose how your city, state, and country will operate.

3. Whose goal is to educate at-risk communities, including returning citizens and, the youth on pertinent issues that will impact their future, as well as increase voters' registration and participation through grassroots lobbying, educational seminars, and citizen advocacy.

     City Hall   RNC   DNC

     1 Vote Counts   NAACP   ACLU

Section 2: Multiple Choice

Please complete each question by circling the BEST ANSWER possible.

1. For your convenience, any registered Pennsylvania voter has the freedom to _____ in an election without providing a reason.

a) march   **b)** vote by mail in ballot

c) democracy   **d)** debate

2. The Polls are open in the state of Pennsylvania from

a) 9 a.m. 5 p.m.   **b)** 6 a.m. to 6 p.m.

c) 8 a.m. to 8 p. m.   **d)** 7 a.m. to 8 p.m.

Section :3 Circle Yes or No

1. Individuals who are on probation or released on parole

Yes or No

2. Incarcerated individuals convicted of misdemeanors can vote with a mail in ballot

Yes or No

3. Individuals who are under house arrest can vote with a mail in ballot

Yes or No

4. Individuals being held while awaiting trial vote with a mail in ballot

Yes or No

5. Individuals on pre-release/halfway house can vote

Yes or No

List The Seven reasons Why You Must Vote

1 _____

2 _____

3 _____

4 _____

5 _____

6 _____

7 _____

Conclusion

So, now that you have studied U.S. Government and the importance of your civic engagement; we hope you will become fully involved in the electoral process. Your vote is your voice as well as, your personal political power. Although voting is a civil right for all US citizens, there are some who still attempt to suppress the Black vote and in general, people of color.

When you do not vote, you engage in self-suppression. **So please...**

Vote because it is a fundamental process and right of yours to decide who best represents you.

Vote because it keeps our system of democracy and leadership working on our behalf!

Vote and do not allow anyone or anything silence you!

Remember when we unite, raise our voices and vote, we can change the future of our community, city, state, and country.

So... make your voice heard and exercise your right to Vote!

Give Back | Get Involved

Dauphin County Community Resources

1 Vote Counts Inc.

https://www.1votecounts.org/

Jones Resources

http://www.jonesresource.org/

The American Red Cross

https://www.redcross.org/local/pennsylvania/greater-pennsylvania/about-us/locations/central-pennsylvania.html

The Big Brothers Big Sisters

https://harrisburgpa.gov/big-brothers-big-sisters/

The United Way

https://www.uwcr.org/

The Salvation Army

https://pa.salvationarmy.org/harrisburg-pa/locations

Tri County Community Action

https://cactricounty.org/

The Foundation for Enhancing Communities

https://www.tfec.org/our-community/initiatives/

The Boys and Girls Club

https://harrisburgpa.gov/boys-girls-club/

The YMCA

https://www.ymca.org/locations/harrisburg-area-metropolitan-ymca

The YWCA

http://www.ywcahbg.org/

The NAACP

https://hbgnaacp.com/

The Urban League

https://greatnonprofits.org/org/urban-league-of-metropolitan-harrisburg-inc

GLOSSARY OF TERMS

House Legislative Calendars

The Union Calendar

A list of all bills that address money and may be considered by the House of Representatives. Generally, bills contained in the Union Calendar can be categorized as appropriations bills or bills raising revenue.

The House Calendar

A list of all the public bills that do not address money and maybe considered by the House of Representatives.

The Corrections Calendar

A list of bills selected by the Speaker of the House in consultation with the Minority leader that will be considered in the House and debated for one hour. Generally, bills are selected because they focus on changing laws, rules and regulations that are judged to be outdated or unnecessary. A 3/5 majority of those present and voting is required to pass bills on the Corrections Calendar.

The Private Calendar

A list of all the private bills that are to be considered by the House. It is called on the first and third Tuesday of every month.

Types of Legislation

Bills

A legislative proposal that if passed by both the House and the Senate and approved by the President becomes law. Each bill is assigned a bill number. HR denotes bills that originate in the House and S denotes bills that originate in the Senate.

Private Bill

A bill that is introduced on behalf of a specific individual that if it is enacted into law only affects the specific person or organization the bill concerns. Often, private bills address immigration or naturalization issues.

Public Bill

A bill that affects the general public if enacted into law.

Simple Resolution

A type of legislation designated by H Res or S Res that is used primarily to express the sense of the chamber where it is introduced or passed. It only has the force of the chamber passing the resolution. A simple resolution is not signed by the President and cannot become public law.

Concurrent Resolutions

A type of legislation designated by H Con Res or S Con Res that is often used to express the sense of both chambers, to set annual budget or to fix adjournment dates. Concurrent resolutions are not signed by the President and therefore do not hold the weight of law.

Joint Resolutions

A type of legislation designated by H J Res or S J Res that is treated the same as a bill unless it proposes an amendment to the Constitution. In this case, 2/3 majority of those present and voting in both the House and the Senate and 3/4 ratification of the states are required for the Constitutional amendment to be adopted.

Other Terms

Calendar Wednesday

A procedure in the House of Representatives during which each standing committees may bring up for consideration any bill that has been reported on the floor on or before the previous day. The procedure also limits debate for each subject matter to two hours.

Cloture

A motion generally used in the Senate to end a filibuster. Invoking cloture requires a vote by 3/5 of the full Senate. If cloture is invoked further debate is limited to 30 hours, it is not a vote on the passage of the piece of legislation.

Committee of The Whole

A committee including all members of the House. It allows bills and resolutions to be considered without adhering to all the formal rules of a House session, such as needing a quorum of 218. All measures on the Union Calendar must be considered first by the Committee of the Whole.

Co-Sponsor

A member or members that add his or her name formally in support of another member's bill. In the House a member can become a co-sponsor of a bill at any point up to the time the last authorized committee considers it. In the Senate a member can become a co-sponsor of a bill any time before the vote takes place on the bill. However, a co-sponsor is not required and therefore, not every bill has a co-sponsor or co-sponsors.

Discharge Petition

A petition that if signed by a majority of the House, 218 members, requires a bill to come out of a committee and be moved to the floor of the House.

Filibuster

An informal term for extended debate or other procedures used to prevent a vote on a bill in the Senate.

Germane

Relevant to the bill or business either chamber is addressing. The House requires an amendment to meet a standard of relevance, being germane, unless a special rule has been passed.

Hopper

Box on House Clerk's desk where members deposit bills and resolutions to introduce them.

Morning Hour

A 90-minute period on Mondays and Tuesdays in the House of Representatives set aside for five-minute speeches by members who have reserved a spot in advance on any topic.

Motion to Recommit

A motion that requests a bill be sent back to committee for further consideration. Normally, the motion is accompanied by instructions concerning what the committee should change in the legislation or general instructions such as that the committee should hold further hearings.

Motion to Table

A motion that is not debatable and that can be made by any Senator or Representative on any pending question. Agreement to the motion is equivalent to defeating the question tabled.

Quorum

The number of Representatives or Senators that must be present before business can begin. In the House 218 members must be present for a quorum. In the Senate 51 members must be present however, Senate can conduct daily business without a quorum unless it is challenged by a point of order.

Rider

An informal term for an amendment or provision that is not relevant to the legislation where it is attached.

Sponsor

The original member who introduces a bill.

Substitute Amendment

An amendment that would replace existing language of a bill or another amendment with its own.

Suspension of the Rules

A procedure in the House that limits debate on a bill to 40 minutes, bars amendments to the legislation and requires a 2/3 majority of those present and voting for the measure to be passed.

Veto

A power that allows the President, a Governor or a Mayor to refuse approval of a piece of legislation. Federally, a President returns a vetoed bill to the Congress, generally with a message. Congress can

Post Assessment Test

1. What did the Declaration of Independence do?

_____

_____

_____

_____

2. Who was the first African American President

_____

_____

_____

_____

3. Who signs federal bills to become laws?

_____

_____

_____

_____

4. What are the two major political parties in the United States?

_____

_____

_____

_____

5. What are two ways that Americans can participate in their democracy?

_____

_____

_____

_____

6. Who was the primary author of the Declaration of Independence?

_____

_____

_____

_____

7. What did the Emancipation Proclamation do?

_____

_____

_____

_____

8. Who can introduce legislation?

_____

_____

_____

_____

9. How many Senators are in the U.S. Congress?

_____

_____

_____

_____

10. How long is the term for members of the House of Representatives?

_____

_____

_____

_____

11. How many justices serve on the Supreme Court?

_____

_____

_____

_____

BONUS QUESTIONS

12. After the Vice President, who is next in line for the U.S. presidency?

--Secretary of State

--President Pro Tempore of the Senate

--Speaker of the House of Representatives

--Secretary of the Treasury

13. Which one of the following rights is guaranteed by the First Amendment to the U.S. Constitution?

--Protection from unreasonable search and seizure

-- Freedom of Religion, Speech and the Press:

--Right to a speedy trial by jury

JOIN OUR TEAM!

Interested candidates, please respond to join1votecounts@gmail.com

For press and general inquiries, contact our headquarters today:

231 State St. Harrisburg, Pennsylvania 17101

michelle@1votecounts.org

office: 717-712-9525

- o   Facebook.com/1votecounts

- o   Instagram.com/1votescounts

- o   Twitter.com/1votecountsFor

Michelle Mardenborough is committed to protecting diversity and democracy through the vote. My Desire is to Engage, Prepare and Empower the next generation to be knowledgeable, authentic, issue driven leaders who will be positive voices of change in the communities they represent. Michelle is certified in lean six sigma. Her areas of expertise include lean management, service excellence, personal branding, succession planning, and executive coaching. Michelle holds a master's degree in Practical Theology from Oral Roberts University. She is the founder of Infinite Possibilities Inc, A nonprofit organization that empowers women to recognize their potential, purpose and destiny through the Word of God and the power of their faith. Michelle is also the founder and Executive Director of 1Vote Counts, a nonpartisan 501c3 civic engagement organization that protects diversity and democracy. Michelle is a "Call to Action Motivational Speaker, she hosts women's retreats, conferences and symposiums; she is the author of Empowered to Lead Determined to Succeed, a workbook on goal setting and achieving your dreams and Motivating Moments a 21-day transformation journal and devotional workbook.

Printed in the United States
by Baker & Taylor Publisher Services